Box Office

SIMON BIRCH

One person—even a teenager—can have great power and influence to change lives and circumstances in the world. Simon Birch has these qualities; and with Jesus' love and grace, we can do remarkable things.

MULAN

Young Mulan turned the gender roles and stereotypes of her culture upside down. The young heroine found courage and determination to be personal traits, not inherent gender traits. Likewise, God calls us to discover who we are as Christians and what we are to be through love and grace.

THE MASK OF ZORRO

A great number of people have been cheated out of their wealth and land, but there is hope that a leader will come and justice will be served. Those are messages youth will experience from this program based on the adventures of Zorro, the Old Testament Book of Joshua, and the plight of impoverished people everywhere.

Behind the Scenes

Scott Grotewold wouldn't be lion if he said that he wrote *The Lion King II: Simba's Pride* devotion and *The Lion King* program. Scott is senior minister of Collegiate UMC and director of the Wesley Foundation at Iowa State University in Ames.

Ask **Skip Parvin** what dreams may come, and he will likely tell you a dream in which youth are devoted disciples of Jesus Christ. What a pleasant thought! Skip, senior minister of Tuskawilla UMC in Casselberry, Florida, is editor of REEL TO REAL and wrote the programs *What Dreams May Come* and *Pleasantville*.

Peggy Dean is a creator of swashbuckling curriculum for youth. Z latest is *The Mask of Zorro*. Peggy, former English teacher and full-time freelance writer, lives in Sarasota, Florida.

Tom and Karen Johnson teamed up to write the *Simon Birch* program. Karen is coordinator of a corporate art museum and writes a regular newsletter. Tom is a United Methodist minister and is a faith-based community organizer in the Thibodaux, Louisiana, area.

Steve Case, a ten-year veteran of youth ministry, takes youth on retreat with *Mulan*. The freelance writer serves as director of youth ministry at Sanlando UMC.

LION KING II: SIMBA'S PRIDE

" 'The LORD is slow to anger,
and abounding in steadfast love,
forgiving iniquity and
transgression,
but by no means clearing the
guilty,
visiting the iniquity of the parents
upon the children
to the third and the fourth
generation.' "
Numbers 14:18

Beloved, we are God's children
now; what we will be has not yet
been revealed. What we do know is
this: when he is revealed, we will
be like him, for we will see him as
he is.
1 John 3:2

So God created humankind
in his image,
in the image of God
he created them;
male and female he created them.
Genesis 1:27

"The glory that you have given me
I have given them, so that they
may be one, as we are one, I in
them and you in me, that they may
become completely one."
John 17:22-23a

Kovu is the last cub born to the pride led by Scar prior to his death. Scar had identified Kovu as the heir to the pride's leadership; and Kovu's mother, Zira, has groomed him for this, which she sees as his destiny. She has also infused hatred for Simba and all his pride into her children and the rest of the lions who have been banished by Simba to the Outlands. She envisions Kovu destroying Simba and returning in glory to control the Pridelands.

When Simba meets Kovu, he has his own set of expectations. Although Kovu professes to have left his outcast pride and become a lone rogue, Simba is suspicious. He knows where Kovu comes from; he knows how he was raised. He assumes that he knows his kind. Simba has categorized and pigeon-holed Kovu, based on his assumptions about Kovu's background.

Kiara is a princess; Kovu is a dangerous pariah. We bear a mark, Simba thinks; and it cannot be escaped.

The Old Testament peoples saw ways in which families suffered from generation to generation for the mistakes and sins of the past (Numbers 14:18). This suffering might be due to the consequences of the past actions upon the family, or it might be the influence of the ancestor on his or her descendants. Since a person may have inherited or learned some of a parent's traits, he or she might find himself or herself thinking in similar ways and making similar decisions as the parent, even with the possibility of wrong decisions. Simba understands this, and expects it of Kovu. But heredity and heritage may also work to a person's benefit. Simba tells Kiara, "[Not wanting to be a princess is] like saying you don't want to be a lion. It's in your blood." While *The Lion King* emphasized the way we are challenged to live out our calling, its sequel points out the dark side of that challenge—the possibility that others might be unfairly judged.

Kiara and Kovu ponder the influence of the past on themselves, too. Kiara tells Kovu, "My father says there was a darkness in Scar that he couldn't escape." Kovu replies fearfully, "Maybe that darkness is a part of me too." The church has taught us that each of us has the possibility for sin within us. Paul says it this way in Romans 5:12, "Therefore, just as sin came into the world through one man, and death came through sin, and so death spread to all because all have sinned." We all bear the mark of Adam; that darkness is a part of us too.

But when the Bible tells us its creation story, it says that humans are made in the image of God (Genesis 1:27). The more we are able to be fully ourselves, then, the more we are in God's image. Temptation and sin is what separates us from God and our humanity. Being in closer relationship is what makes us more fully human. The truth is that Kovu initially approaches Simba's pride, intending to kill Simba when they are alone. But by the time Kovu has an opportunity to do so, he is unable. His affection for Kiara, Simba, and the others is too strong.

We become more human and are in closer relationship with God if we stay in contact with people who are themselves human and in close relationship with God. By living near the strong and kind Simba and his pride, Kovu comes to love and appreciate him and his way of life. As followers of Christ, we believe that Jesus is the ultimate one who can restore us and bring us back to the stature of being fully human. We are called into relationship with one who was fully human and very human at the same time that he was fully God and very God.

Simba recognizes the dilemma his judgmentalism creates. On one occasion, he tells Kovu that hatred is a killer. "Scar couldn't let go of his hate, and in the end it killed him." He compares the hate to a fire that has swept through the

land; and he adds, "Sometimes, what's left behind can grow better than the generation before if given the chance." He has hope that Kovu can be different; but coincidences cause him to cling to his earlier suspicions. He lifts his eyes to the heavens and speaks to his father, Mufasa: "Father, I am lost. Kovu is one of them." His mate, Nala, speaks the word that suggests that perhaps Kovu will rise above the expectations of others: "Kiara wants to walk the path expected of her. Perhaps Kovu does not want to walk the path expected of him."

Our destiny is not certain. We do not have to let our heredity, our upbringing, our environment control who we become. It is Jesus Christ who sets us free from that kind of fatalism. As John says in his First Letter, "We are God's children now; what we will be has not yet been revealed. What we do know is this: when he is revealed, we will be like him, for we will see him as he is." (1 John 3:2)

To the end, Zira is unable to let go of her hatred. Her belief in destiny and her refusal to forgive lead to her death. Each of us who has been touched by the love and forgiveness of God will respond in one of the two ways exhibited by the lions in the film: either we will become a reflection of the forgiveness and love that we have experienced, or we will continue on a road to death as we refuse to forgive others as God has forgiven us.

In a rainstorm at the end of the film, all of the other lions come to realize that they are alike in more ways than they are different. Simba admits his judgment of Kovu. There may be applications to the issue of race here. Earlier, the outcast lions seem to have a grayer hue than the brightly-colored lions of the Pridelands; but in the hazy, stormy weather, these differences are not evident. They acknowledge that they are one and that they can live together. Similarly, we share more in common as humans with those

of different race, ethnicity, or background than we do differences. Jesus says that we are one (John 17:22-23). Can we live together?

Pray: "God, help me to know the fullness of your grace in my life so that I may extend that grace to others, not limiting or judging them but restoring my broken relationships and consummating my forgiveness in Christ, through whom I pray. Amen."

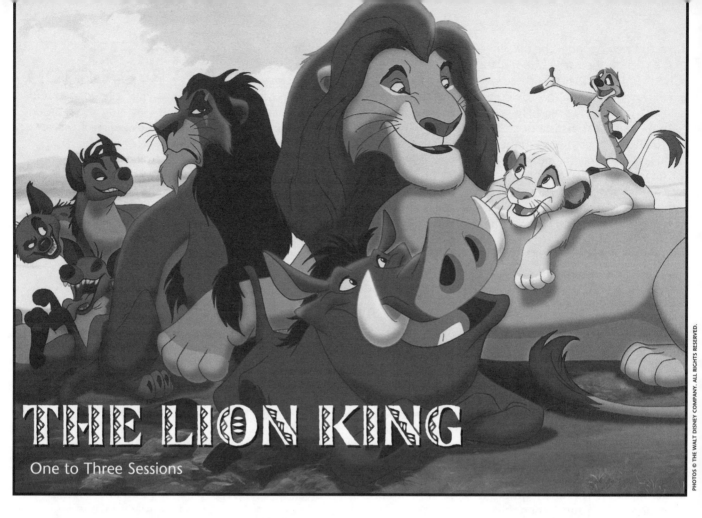

THE LION KING

One to Three Sessions

In those days Jesus came from Nazareth of Galilee and was baptized by John in the Jordan. And just as he was coming up out of the water, he saw the heavens torn apart and the Spirit descending like a dove on him. And a voice came from heaven, "You are my Son, the Beloved; with you I am well pleased."

Mark 1:9-11

THEME

God's call and claim is upon each of us to be more than what we have become. And with God, we are more than we are on our own. In these sessions, youth will explore the idea of being called and will be encouraged to accept their own call.

PURPOSE

The youth will learn about Christian heritage, the ongoing community of faith, and the impact of one's past.

SYNOPSIS

Simba is a lion cub, the heir to the throne held by his father, Mufasa, the lion king. Mufasa's envious brother, Scar, carries out a plot to kill Mufasa and have Simba run away from home in shame. Simba grows to adulthood in exile, befriended by an underachieving meerkat and warthog, Timon and Pumbaa. Meanwhile, the Pridelands are devastated under Scar's leadership. When it is discovered that Simba is still alive, he is called to accept responsibility and return to his homeland to confront Scar.

BACKGROUND

The Lion King (1994) is 88 minutes long and is rated G.

CAUTIONS

There are no cautions, although the depicted death of the young lion cub's father can be traumatic for someone who may have recently lost a loved one.

As always, preview the entire movie and send home a Student Movie Pass (parent consent form on the inside back cover) if you think that is necessary.

MATERIALS

- *The Lion King* video
- VCR and TV
- Bibles
- Pens or pencils
- Photocopies of the "Who Am I?" worksheet
- *The Lion King* soundtrack recording (optional)
- *The Lion King* original Broadway cast recording (optional)

DISCUSSING & LEARNING

**Do not fear, for I have redeemed you;
I have called you
by name, you are mine.
When you pass
through the waters,
I will be with you;
and through the rivers,
they shall not
overwhelm you;
when you walk
through fire you
shall not be burned,
and the flame shall not
consume you.**

**Isaiah 43:1-2
(See also 1 Corinthians 13:11, 1 Peter 2:9, and Galatians 5:13)**

Question 1: Why does Simba say that he just can't wait to be king? How does Simba's understanding of what it means to be the king differ from that of his father, Mufasa?

Answer 1: Simba believes that when he gets to be king, he will be free to do anything he wants whenever he wants; he will be free merely to please himself. The calling of his father is to help Simba understand the responsibility that

VIDEO VIEWING Begin with an opening prayer. Then view scenes from *The Truman Show* where recommended in the program. If you've decided to view clips, use the Video Viewing chart below.

Suggestion: Preview the film on the VCR that you will use with the program. Make note of these key scenes so you can fast forward during the program, using these approximate start-end times and your VCR counter.

Start-End	Event	Count
0:00–0:04	Song: "Circle of Life"; Simba is presented and anointed.	_____
0:07–0:10	Mufasa tells Simba of his legacy and his responsibility.	_____
0:15–0:17	Song: "I Just Can't Wait to Be King"	_____
0:23–0:25	Mufasa tells Simba that his ancestors can always be found in the stars for support.	_____
0:32–0:38	Mufasa dies; Scar encourages Simba to run away.	_____
0:43–0:45	Timon tells Simba to put past behind him: "Hakuna Matata."	_____
0:51–0:53	Simba, Timon, and Pumbaa talk about the stars; Rafiki realizes that Simba is still alive.	_____
0:57–1:00	Nala tells Simba that his being alive is like being "back from the dead." Song: "Can You Feel the Love Tonight"	_____
1:01–1:08	Simba learns several lessons (getting hit with a walking stick is one); Simba decides to return to the Pridelands.	_____
1:11–1:20	The final battle is fought.	_____
1:22–1:23	The Pridelands are restored, and there is a new birth.	_____

comes with freedom. With the power and authority that comes with being the ruler comes also the obligation to do what he can to maintain the fragile balance of life. To be free is to be not confined in being able to give oneself to others.

Question 2: Simba is surprised and amazed to find that Rafiki knows of his father:

Simba: You knew my father?
Rafiki: Correction: I know your father.

Then, as Simba sees his reflection in the water hole, Rafiki says, "You see, he lives in you."

How do your parents live in you?

Answer 2: (personal opinion)

Question 3: When the adult Simba sees Mufasa in the constellation of stars, he hears Mufasa's voice saying to him, "You have forgotten who you are and so have forgotten me. You are more than what you have become. You must take your place in the circle of life. Remember who you are." How is it possible to forget who one is? How does forgetting oneself result in forgetting one's parent as well?

Answer 3: Part of it may be genetic; part of it may be emulation; part of it may be living under the same roof; part of it may be the baggage others place on us.

Whatever it is, it is true that in some way or ways, we do carry some of the same traits as our parents and our ancestors. We bear their image. We represent a legacy that is larger than just our individual selves. When others see us, they may be reminded of one of our parents. This is not just true of our biological heritage or the heritage of our upbringing. It is also to be true of our spiritual heritage (see question 9).

Question 4: Hand out copies of the chart printed below. Read the "Who Are You?" portion of the chart, then have group members fill in the blanks in the "Who Says So?" column, naming different places where each identification may be used.

Answer 4: Answers given in "Who Says So?" below may include (in order) schools, IQ tests; TV, magazines, gym teachers; advertisers, marketers; pop music, *Beverly Hills 90210,* secular society, and self-help books. One response to the last statement should certainly be The Church. (If it's not, we're proclaiming our message poorly!)

In the midst of all of the other voices telling us who we are, it is easy to miss the voice of the church calling to us. The church is here to remind us that someone greater

- - - - - - - - - - - - - - - - - - *Cut here before giving this activity sheet to the youth.* - - - - - - - - - - - - - - - - - -

LEARNING ACTIVITY 1: WHO AM I?

Searching for our identity consumes much of our time. There are endless groups, causes, and cults ready to tell us who we are. Where might you find yourself identified in these ways?

WHO ARE YOU?

You are primarily your brain. You are mostly a rational, thinking, reasoning being who absorbs facts and figures. Learning to live will come later. For now, you are living to learn. Who you are is defined by what you know.

You are a physical being. Your body is your most important possession. So take care of it, nurture it, love it, develop it, display it, and show it off.

You are a consumer, a maker and spender of money. You are a capitalist; doer; producer; obtainer of stereo, nice clothes, and the car of your dreams—all in preparation for your first mortgage with a two-car garage and 30 years of payments.

You are a competitor. Goal Number One: Win! You work out, practice, study plays, and prepare for every game. When you win, you are on top of the world. When you lose, that world crumbles on top of you.

You are an autonomous, self-made individual. Nobody will look out for you but you. You are the most important project in your life, so look out for Number One: you. Nurture, satisfy, soothe, make happy, thrill, and love yourself.

You are baptized. You are someone to whom a name has been given: *Christian.* You are one who has been claimed by God. You are one of the chosen; you are royalty.

WHO SAYS SO?

_____

_____

_____

_____

_____

_____

_____

_____

_____

_____

_____

_____

_____

_____

_____

LASTING IMAGES

The Bible contains many powerful images as it tells the story of the people of faith. Were the creators of *The Lion King* influenced by these themes in their making of the movie? Did they draw on some of these images as they told the story of Simba? Have the youht look up and read some of the suggested Bible verses listed below. Then ask the youth if the verse reminds them of any of the scenes in *The Lion King*.

THE SCRIPTURE	THE BIBLE STORY	THE LION KING
Matthew 2:2, 11	The Wise Men bow in homage in the presence of the young Jesus.	The animals of the jungle gather to bow in tribute at Simba's birth.
Luke 2:22, 28-32	Jesus is presented in the Temple.	The young lion is lifted to the heavens.
Luke 2:40; Mark 6:3	Jesus grows up strong; he learns the carpenter's trade.	Simba is trained by his father, Mufasa, in hunting and leadership.
Matthew 2:13-15	Joseph takes Jesus to Egypt to protect him from Herod.	Young Simba has to flee the wrath of Scar.
Genesis 21:10, 14-20	Ishmael is banished from his home and grows up in the wilderness.	Simba banishes himself from his homeland and grows up in the wilderness.
Luke 4:1-12	Jesus is tempted by Satan in the wilderness; the temptations are self-gratification, power, security.	The evil Scar conveys a selfish view of life to Simba; Simba's life in the wilderness is self-centered.
Genesis 45:25-26	Jacob learns that his son, Joseph, whom he thought was dead, is alive.	After thinking Simba long-dead, Nala his own mother learn that he is alive.
Matthew 3:1-4	A description of John the Baptist, a holy man of the wilderness, proclaiming a call to repent and to accept responsibility.	Rafiki is the religious figure in this piece, living in the wilderness and calling Simba to repent and accept responsibility.
Mark 1:9-11	Jesus is baptized by John; a voice from heaven calls Jesus and claims him.	Rafiki anoints the young cup; later, at the water hole, Simba hears his father's voice.
Luke 15:1-20	The Parable of the Prodigal Son.	After a selfish period, Simba "comes to his senses" and decides to return home.
Isaiah 43:1-3	"I have called you by name; you are mine; I am with you."	Mufasa (in the stars) gives Simba these same assurances.
1 Kings 18-20	Elijah is banished from his homeland but returns to confront the evil powers.	Simba lives in exile, but returns to his homeland to confront the evil powers.

than us has named us and claimed us and seeks us and loves us. We are children of God and heirs, even to life eternal.

Question 5: What does *Hakuna Matata* mean? How do the two words express Timon and Pumbaa's philosophy of life? How does Simba's acceptance of this philosophy cause him to "forget who he is"?

Answer 5: *Hakuna Matata* means "No worries for the rest of your days." Timon and Pumbaa live in the moment, not worrying about the past, not making plans for the future. They have no worries. When Simba embraces this lifestyle for himself, he enters his own little world, forgetting his father's lessons that the pride is depending on him.

CLOSING PRAYER

Lead the youth in the following prayer:

"We are a part of your people, O God. We are some of those you have named, called, and set apart for service in the name of Christ. We thank you, God

- that you have given us special gifts and abilities to share with others.
- that we have an identity as your children, precious and honored in your sight.
- that though we may forget who we are and whose we are, you never forget us, and our names are forever written on your heart.

Amen."

LEARNING ACTIVITY 2

A stage version of *The Lion King* opened on Broadway in New York City in 1997. The show includes the same songs as in the movie, but it has several new songs written especially for the stage show. The new songs, "They Live in You," "Endless Night," and "Shadowland" especially deal with some of the themes of this study. You may want to acquire the original cast recording and play these new songs for your group, listening for their messages and gaining new insights.

LEARNING ACTIVITY 3

Watch the scene early in the film where Mufasa is training Simba to hunt and teaching him about the dependence of each species in the jungle upon the others. Have someone who is particularly interested in environmental stewardship give a report to the group on the balance of nature—the circle of life.

Question 6: Why do the Pridelands fall into devastation under Scar's reign? What was different under Mufasa's rule?

Answer 6: Mufasa's reign is marked by love and gentleness; but Mufasa also recognizes that being firm and strict may also be required to keep the kingdom functioning properly and balanced. Scar, on the other hand, is quite the opposite. He rules with cruelty and harshness. Meanwhile, his relaxed attitude toward responsibility results in an anything goes mentality; and the Pridelands suffer.

Question 7: What is Rafiki's purpose? Who serves the same purpose as Rafiki in your life?

Answer 7: Rafiki is the prophet of this film, calling Simba to responsibility and speaking the truth even though Simba would rather not hear it. Rafiki is the historian, remembering the old tales and reminding Simba of his place in the unfolding story. Rafiki is the wise old mentor, teaching the deeper lessons of life that come from experience.

Question 8: Watch the scene again where Rafiki hits Simba with his walking stick. When Simba protests, Rafiki says, "It doesn't matter; it's in the past!" Earlier, Timon teaches Simba, "You've got to put your past behind you." How do these two statements differ?

Answer 8: When Timon says, "You've got to put your past behind you," he speaks the truth, but he misses the further truth that you can't run from or forget your past. We are the result of our past. As Rafiki says, "The past can hurt. The way I see it, you can either run from it or learn from it." That Simba learns this lesson is shown when Rafiki swings his stick again, and Simba ducks. Maybe Pumbaa is closer to the truth than Timon when he mixes up the phrase saying, "You've got to put your behind in your past."

Question 9: How are you like the lion king? By virtue of your baptism, to what responsibility are you called?

Answer 9: The children of the King are to recognize that we bear the stamp of the image of God. We are called to come out from our private lives of self-indulgence and selfishness and claim our inheritance. God, through Christ, always calls us to serve the needs of God's realm.

Question 10: Scar asks, "Must it always end in violence?" Why do you think so many people think that violence is the solution to their problems?

LEARNING ACTIVITY 4

Invite your pastor to discuss the meaning of the sacrament of baptism. For purposes of your discussion of *The Lion King,* ask your pastor to focus especially on the implications of baptism regarding

- receiving the name *Christian* and being welcomed into a family;
- the congregation's vow or vows and their responsibility in the baptism;
- the placing of a claim and a call on a person's life.

LEARNING ACTIVITY 5

At a meeting of your group, just before a baptism is to take place in worship, go through the order of worship for the baptism as it is printed in the hymnal or book of worship. Call special attention to each movement or significant part having to do with call, taking responsibility, and becoming a part of the family of faith.

GOD'S CALL TO INDIVIDUALS

The Bible contains many reports of God's call to individuals and many different responses to that call. Have group members look up different biblical figures from the lists below and answer these questions:

- How did God's call come to the individual? To what task is the person called?
- How did the person respond? To what extent was the person confident, hesitant, willing, or uncertain?
- In what ways does God or Jesus offer reassurance to the person called?
- How might you have responded if you had been in the person's situation?

OLD TESTAMENT

Abraham (Genesis 12:1-9)
Abraham and Sarah (Genesis 17:1-21)
Jacob (Genesis 32:22-23)
Moses (Exodus 3:1–4:20)
Joshua (Joshua 1)
Deborah (Judges 4:4-22)
Gideon (Judges 6:11-18)
Hannah and Samuel (1 Samuel 1:1–4:1)
Elijah (1 Kings 17:1–19:21)
Naomi and Ruth (Ruth 1:1-18)
Isaiah (Isaiah 6)
Jeremiah (Jeremiah 1:4-19)
Ezekiel (Ezekiel 1-3)
Hosea (Hosea 1:1-11)
Amos (Amos 1:1-2, 7:7-17)
Zechariah (Zechariah 7)

NEW TESTAMENT

Zecharias and Elizabeth (Luke 1)
Mary (Luke 1)
Joseph (Matthew 1)
John the Baptiser (Luke 3:1-20)
Jesus (Matthew 3-4)
Jesus (Mark 1:9-12)
Jesus (Luke 3:21–4:21)
Peter (Luke 5:1-11)
Matthew (Matthew 9:9-13)
Paul (Acts 9)
Paul (Galatians 1)
Timothy (2 timothy 3:10–4:5)
Titus (Titus 2)
A ruler (Luke 18:18-30)
Zacchaeus (Luke 19:1-10)
Nicodemus (John 3:1-21)

Pleasantville

Two or Three Sessions

> But law came in, with the result that the trespass multiplied; but where sin increased, grace abounded all the more, so that, just as sin exercised dominion in death, so grace might also exercise dominion through justification leading to eternal life through Jesus Christ our Lord.
> What then are we to say? Should we continue in sin in order that grace may abound? By no means! How can we who died to sin go on living in it?
>
> Romans 5:20-6:2

PURPOSE

Youth will explore the relationship between sin and grace when free will is introduced into a predetermined world.

THEME

Free will brings out the best and the worst of human nature, but even when we are at our worst God still reaches out to us with love.

BACKGROUND

Pleasantville is 124 minutes long and is rated PG-13.

CAUTIONS

Pleasantville is rated PG-13 primarily because it presents some mature sexual themes. There are a few slips in language, implied sexual relationships, and a discussion between the sitcom mom and her daughter that leads to her discovering her own sexuality.

SYNOPSIS

When a nineties brother and sister fight over a remote control, they are magically transported into the predetermined, "rerun" world of a fifties family sitcom. In the process of adjusting to their life in the new environment and attempting to get back home, they introduce free will into the deterministic sitcom world, with chaotic results. As they teach the characters in Pleasantville to deal with their new-found free will and individuality, they learn significant lessons about themselves, which change their lives forever.

MATERIALS

- *Pleasantville* video
- TV and VCR
- Chalkboard and chalk or newsprint and markers.
- Be sure that you have gathered all materials necessary for any of the suggested activities provided with the sessions.

VIDEO VIEWING

VIDEO VIEWING After an opening prayer, show *Pleasantville*. If you have time only for clips, key scenes are identified below. Use the Video Viewing chart for quickly locating these clips during discussion.

Suggestion: Preview the film on the VCR that you will use with the session. Make note of these key scenes so you can fast forward during the session, using these approximate start times and your VCR counter.

Start	Event	Count
0:02	Depressing facts about living in the nineties	_____
0:09	TV repairman appears.	_____
0:13	Transported into the TV	_____
0:26	Mr. Johnson just keeps wiping.	_____
0:31	Lover's Lane	_____
0:36	Skip sees one red rose.	_____
0:41	"It never changes. It never gets any better or any worse."	_____
0:49	"I baked them for you."	_____
0:51	"What's outside of Pleasantville?"	_____
0:57	Mom becomes colorized; Bud helps her cover it with makeup.	_____
1:00	Art Book: "Where am I going to see colors like that?"	_____
1:07	Mr. Johnson washes off Betty's gray.	_____
1:11	Apple: Garden of Eden	_____
1:13	Dad comes home; mom's not there. He's lost.	_____
1:16	Meeting at the bowling alley, real rain	_____
1:24	Prejudice against "the coloreds"	_____
1:27	"You don't deserve paradise!"	_____
1:28	David defends his "sitcom" mom.	_____
1:33	Second town meeting	_____
1:37	"I don't know what I would do if I couldn't paint."	_____
1:41	The trial	_____
1:48	Goodbyes: Jennifer goes to college; David returns home.	_____
1:53	David realizes how much his real mom needs him.	_____

USING THESE SESSIONS & ACTIVITIES

If you have time, show the entire film before beginning the discussion and activities. Review key scenes, if necessary, during activities that emphasize those scenes. If you have time only for clips, be prepared to provide an account of the missing story parts so that the narrative continuity is maintained.

ICEBREAKER

Ask the youth the following:

Question 1: If you could magically enter into any television show, which show would it be? Why?

Question 2: What character or type of character would you be?

Question 3: Would your character's personality change the world? If so, how?

DISCUSSING & LEARNING

Before beginning this discussion, show the clip labeled "Depressing facts about living in the nineties."

Question 1: How does this list of depressing facts about the nineties make you feel about the world in which you live?

Question 2: Why do you think David spends so much time watching *Pleasantville*? (He wants to escape, to deny, to avoid the pain in his everyday existence. Being good at *Pleasantville* trivia helps him with his low self-esteem.)

Question 3: What are Jennifer's (David's sister's) problems? (has low self-esteem, needs to be popular, uses her sexuality to get attention)

Before asking the following questions, show the clips labeled "TV repairman appears" and "Transported into the TV."

Question 4: Why does the TV repairman choose David? (He believes that he will "fit" in Pleasantville, he wants to help him escape, he knows that a trip to Pleasantville will help David learn what he needs to know about himself in order to change his life.)

Question 5: The TV repairman says: "I know how I would feel if mine [his TV] went out—like losing a friend." Have you ever felt this way about television? Do you know someone who feels this way about television? How important is television to you?

Question 6: When David and Jennifer are transported into the TV, the repairman calls it a miracle. Do you agree with him? Does this qualify as a miracle?

Show all or some of the following clips: "Mr. Johnson just keeps wiping," "Lover's Lane," "Skip sees one red rose," "It never changes. It never gets any better or any worse," "I baked them for you," "What's outside of Pleasantville?" Make sure that you have access to a chalkboard and chalk or newsprint and markers. List the responses as the youth suggest them.

Question 7: What are some of the advantages to living in Pleasantville before David and Jennifer's action

BLACK AND WHITE PARTY

Have a Black and White Party. Have everyone dress in black and white, decorate the room in black and white, and serve only black and white food. Divide the youth into smaller groups and have them put gray make up on a volunteer to see who can create the best black and white character.

You could also have a Fabulous Fifties or Pleasantville party. Have the youth dress in fifties styles, dance to fifties music, and have fifties movies playing on a TV. You could also have the youth dress as their favorite characters from *Pleasantville,* and award prizes for those who look most like the characters from the movie.

Have a Black and White TV Night. Check out copies of episodes from *Leave it to Beaver, My Three Sons,* and *Father Knows Best.* Show them to the youth and discuss them.

changed it? (Possible answers may include but are not limited to the following: no crime; no need for toilets; the basketball team never loses; you can eat all you want and never get fat; no sex, which means no need to worry about making sexually-related decisions; everybody is pleasant; no fires; everybody looks good; no pain; no suffering; no homelessness; everyone gets along; no prejudice.)

Question 8: What are some of the disadvantages to living in Pleasantville before David and Jennifer's actions changed it? (Possible answers may include but are not limited to the following: nothing ever changes; you're stuck being a "nerd" all of your life; no color; no art; no great literature; no real love with all of its complications; because the basketball team never loses, they don't truly understand the joy of winning; you have to live the same days and events over and over again; the music in the jukebox never changes; no variety in food or experience.)

Show some of the following clips: "Mom becomes colorized; Bud helps her cover it with makeup"; "Art Book: "Where am I going to see colors like that?"; "Mr. Johnson washes off Betty's gray"; "What's outside of Pleasantville?"; "Dad comes home; mom's not there; he's lost"; "Meeting at the bowling alley—real rain"; "Prejudice against 'the coloreds' "; "David defends his 'sitcom' mom"; "second town

meeting"; "I don't know what I would do if I couldn't paint." Continue to record answers to these questions on the chalkboard or the newsprint.

Question 9: What are some of the positive changes that take place in Pleasantville after David and Jennifer introduce the residents to free will? (Possible answers may include but are not limited to the following: Mr. Johnson discovers his talent for art, the mother discovers that she is completely unfulfilled and begins to make a life for herself, the books at the library fill in with great literature, color is introduced to the world, the father learns how to express his love, David learns to be assertive, Jennifer learns that she is intelligent and goes to college, people are able to express their joy in living.)

Question 10: What are some of the negative changes that take place in Pleasantville after David and Jennifer introduce the residents to free will? (Possible answers may include but are not limited to the following: hatred, prejudice, violence, confusion, sexual promiscuity, censorship, intolerance, mob mentality.)

Show the following clips: "Apple: Garden of Eden" and "You don't deserve paradise!" Read Genesis 3:1-14 (the Garden of Eden).

Question 11: How is the situation in Pleasantville similar to the situation in the Garden of Eden? (The people choose to have free will and become disobedient.)

Question 12: The TV repairman tells David, "You don't deserve paradise." Do you think that human beings deserve paradise?

Question 13: Would you want to live in paradise if the price you had to pay was giving up your free will?

Ask a youth to read aloud Romans 5:20–6:2. Then use the following questions to focus the discussion:

Question 14: What do you think Paul means when he says, "where sin increased, grace abounded all the more"? (Paul is demonstrating that if we never had free will, then grace would be neither possible nor necessary. The joy of receiving and knowing God's forgiving grace is dependent on our having the weakness that leads us to sin and need for forgiveness.)

Question 15: What do you think Paul means when he says, "Should we continue in sin in order that grace may abound?" (Paul's opponents had suggested that Paul was teaching people to go ahead and sin so that they could experience grace more fully. Paul challenges this interpretation by suggesting that even though sin leads to the beautiful experience of grace, when we ask for forgiveness, we do not want to continue to be slaves to our sin.)

Question 16: What do you think Paul means when he says, "How can we who died to sin go on living in it?" (For Paul, continuing to live in sin was a betrayal of the love of God in Jesus Christ. No Christian should ever depend on God's grace while he or she continues to live in sin. God has allowed us free will in order to deny the power sin has over us by choosing Jesus Christ and salvation.)

Question 17: Can you tie this Scripture to what happens in Pleasantville? (Before free will, Pleasantville was a kind of paradise, but the people did not have the opportunity to make the choices that determined the direction their lives would take. One of the ironies of grace is that we have to make wrong choices, fail, and sin before we can experience the complete joy of grace.)

Question 18: List examples of grace at work in and through Pleasantville? (Answers may include but are not limited to the following: David discovers his inner strength and how much his "real world" mom needs him; Jennifer discovers her inner strength and goes to college; Mr. Johnson discovers his artistic talent and learns to express it responsibly; the mother discovers that she is unfulfilled and begins to question her relationship with her husband, but then she realizes that she must make a decision because her life affects other people (her husband and Mr. Johnson); the father learns that he really loves his wife, and if he wants to keep her, he must be willing to change.)

What Dreams May Come

Two to Four Sessions

"To die, to sleep; to sleep:
perchance to dream: ay, there's
the rub;
for in that sleep of death what
dreams may come?"

**William Shakespeare's *Hamlet*:
Act III, Scene I**

PURPOSE
Youth will explore their own ideas about heaven, hell, and the afterlife in relation to the film and to Scripture.

THEME
Heaven and hell belong to God just as much as any part of God's creation does, and our understanding of the afterlife will be limited until we can actually experience it.

BACKGROUND
What Dreams May Come is 106 minutes long and is rated PG-13.

CAUTIONS
What Dreams May Come is rated PG-13 mostly for thematic elements that involve death and graphic (and potentially disturbing) depictions of hell. There are a few slips in language and a moment of partial nudity (Annie diving in to go skinny dipping).

SYNOPSIS
When physician Chris Nielsen stops to help at the scene of an automobile accident, he himself dies when another car skids out of control. Guided by his dead son, daughter, and former mentor, Chris experiences the transition into heaven and begins to gain new insights about the afterlife and about himself. Despite the fact that he finds great joy in his new existence, he doesn't feel complete without his wife, Annie, whom he feels is his soul mate. When she commits suicide in her grief over losing Chris, she is trapped in hell by her own sense of hopelessness. Chris vows to find her and bring her back from hell to heaven.

MATERIALS
• *What Dreams May Come* video
• TV and VCR
• chalkboard and chalk or newsprint and markers.

USING THESE SESSIONS & ACTIVITIES
If yo have time, show the entire film before beginning the discussion and activities. Review key scenes, if necessary, during activities that emphasize those scenes. If you have time for clips,

be prepared to provide an account of the missing story parts so that the narrative continuity is maintained.

SESSION 1: THE DENIAL OF DEATH

So it is with the resurrection of the dead. What is sown is perishable, what is raised is imperishable. It is sown in dishonor, it is raised in glory. It is sown in weakness, it is raised in power. It is sown a physical body, it is raised a spiritual body.
1 Corinthians 15:42

(See also 1 Corinthians 15:43-55)

DISCUSSING & LEARNING

Before beginning this discussion, read aloud 1 Corinthians 15:42-55.

View any or all of the following clips: "Chris dies," "Doc's first visit," "Putting the dog to sleep," "Chris tries to communicate by forcing Annie to write his thoughts," and "Graveyard: 'It's over when you stop wanting her.'"

Question 1: After Chris dies, Doc comes to escort him to heaven. Why do you think Chris stays in the world to watch rather than immediately going to heaven? (He doesn't accept the fact that he is dead. He doesn't want to leave Annie.)

Question 2: Do you think that all human beings deny death (not only the deaths of others but their own death)? Why do you think we do this? Are you comfortable with the idea of death?

VIDEO VIEWING Begin with an opening prayer. Then view *What Dreams May Come*. If time is short, the clips the Video Viewing chart below provide a good idea of the story line.

Suggestion: Preview the film on the VCR that you will use with the sessions. Make note of these key scenes so that you can fast forward during the session, using these approximate start times and your VCR counter.

Start	Event	Count
0:11	Chris dies.	_____
0:12	Doc's first visit	_____
0:15	Putting the dog to sleep	_____
0:21	Chris tries to communicate by forcing Annie to write his thoughts.	_____
0:22	Graveyard: "It's over when you stop wanting her."	_____
0:24	Chris enters heaven (one of his wife's paintings).	_____
0:30	The nature of Heaven is described to Chris.	_____
0:34	The tree Annie paints appears in Chris's heaven.	_____
0:38	Chris defines "soul mates."	_____
0:43	Chris's daughter comes to him in a different form.	_____
0:52	Annie commits suicide.	_____
0:59	Chris meets the tracker.	_____
1:08	"If I was going through hell I would want only one person by my side."	_____
1:11	Chris recognizes Ian.	_____
1:14	Chris talks Annie out of the mental institution.	_____
1:16	Sea of frozen faces	_____
1:22	Chris recognizes Albert.	_____
1:30	Chris says goodbye to his mentor as he decides to stay with Annie in hell.	_____
1:39	Annie finally recognizes Chris in hell.	_____
1:40	Chris and Annie are reunited in heaven.	_____

Question 3: Would any of you care to tell us a personal story of how you felt when someone close to you died? (Please ensure that the group will be open minded and sensitive to those who choose to tell their stories.)

Question 4: When does Chris realize that he cannot stay with Annie and continue in his denial? (When they are in the graveyard, Doc says to Chris, "It's over when you stop wanting her." Chris touches Annie to reassure her, and she recoils and begins to cry. This is the point when Chris realizes that he must leave Annie behind and move on to whatever is next.)

Question 5: How does our Scripture lesson from 1 Corinthians speak to the denial of death? (Paul emphasizes the need for a transition from physical existence to spiritual existence. He says that we don't understand exactly what form this spiritual existence will take, but we will be with Christ.)

SESSION 2: THE NATURE OF HEAVEN

But our citizenship is in heaven, and it is from there that we are expecting a Savior, the Lord Jesus Christ.

Philippians 3:20

DISCUSSING & LEARNING

Before beginning this discussion, read Philippians 3:20.

View any or all of the following clips in which Chris enters heaven (one of his wife's paintings), the nature of heaven is described to Chris, and the tree Annie paints appears in Chris's heaven.

BEFORE THE SESSION

Before the youth arrive, write the following quotations from the movie on posterboard or newsprint sheets as large as possible and tape them up strategically around the room. (You could have the youth do this themselves as they arrive.)

"I screwed up; I'm in Dog Heaven."

"The place where we all go can't be bad, can it, girl?"

"We all paint our own surroundings."

"You're creating a whole world from your imagination."

"We see what we choose to see."

"This is real. Physical is the illusion."

"Your brain is just meat; it rots and disappears."

"Time does not exist here."

"Here is big enough for everyone to have his own private universe."

"Is this where we go when we die?"

"I didn't look like this in the body, you know."

Use the quotations to begin discussions. Then ask the following questions:

Question 1: What is heaven like for Chris? (He finds himself in one of Annie's paintings. He is creating heaven from his imagination.)

Question 2: What would heaven be like for you if you were creating it from your own imagination?

Question 3: Do you like the idea that heaven is created from our imagination, or do you think that it will take another form?

Question 4: Does Paul think that we will create our own heaven from our imagination? (Paul admits that he doesn't know what heaven will be like, or for that matter, that any human being can know what heaven will be like. But he does know that it will be a special place of the spirit.)

Question 5: How do you feel about Paul's idea of a spiritual body? What do you think it will be like?

There are two significant problems with this view of heaven presented by *What Dreams May Come*. 1) heaven is created by the individual for the individual. In Christian theology, heaven is not created for us; it is created by God and for God. We are part of that creation. We believe that heaven is a celebration of the lordship and love of God. It is God that determines what heaven is like, not us. 2) God is hardly present at all in this movie. God gets one passing mention when Chris asks, "Where is God in all this?" And Doc answers, "He's up there somewhere, shouting down that he loves us." Point these problems out to the youth and then ask the following questions:

Question 6: Would heaven be incomplete for you without a direct encounter with Jesus and God?

Question 7: Do you think that God is present in Chris' heaven even though God isn't mentioned much? How?

Question 8: If you think that heaven will be different than it is in this film, what will it be like?

Question 9: What do you think our Scripture means when it says we are born to be "citizens of heaven"?

ACTIVITY: WHAT'S YOUR HEAVEN?

Have each youth create his or her own heaven from his or her own imagination. What would it be like? What would you need to have there?

Who would you want to be there? Who would you want to be your guide? Encourage the youth to be creative—to write, draw, paint, sculpt, dance, or act out what he or she envisions.

SESSION 3: DEALING WITH HELL

Do not fear those who kill the body but cannot kill the soul; rather fear him who can destroy both soul and body in hell.

Matthew 10:28

CAUTION

This session deals with two of the most traumatic ideas for youth: hell and suicide. Take great care to be sensitive to the feelings such discussions will create for the individuals participating.

DISCUSSING & LEARNING

Before beginning this discussion, read aloud Matthew 10:28 and Psalm 139:7-12.

View any or all of the following clips: "Chris meets the tracker, 'If I was going through hell, I would want only one person by my side,'" "Chris recognizes Ian," "Chris talks Annie out of the mental institution," "Sea of frozen faces," "Chris recognizes Albert," "Chris says goodbye to his mentor as he decides to stay with Annie in hell," "Annie finally recognizes Chris in hell," and "Chris and Annie are reunited in heaven."

BEFORE THE SESSION

Before the youth arrive, write the following quotations from the film on posterboard or newsprint sheets

as large as possible and tape them up strategically around the room. (You could have the youth do this themselves as they arrive.)

"She's a suicide. Suicides go somewhere else."

"Hell is for those who don't know they're dead."

"Each of has an instant where we realize that there is a natural order to our existence."

"It's not all fire and pain. The real hell is your life gone wrong."

"It's not about understanding; it's about not giving up."

"No one has ever seen a suicide brought back."

"Nothing will break her denial; it is stronger than her love."

"In hell, there is the danger of losing your mind."

"I believe if I was going through hell I would only want one person by my side."

"Suicides punish themselves."

"Good people end up in hell because they can't forgive themselves."

"Sometimes when you lose, you win."

"Never give up."

Use the quotations to begin discussions. Then ask the following questions:

Question 1: How do you feel about Annie ending up in hell after she commits suicide?

Question 2: Do you think that hell will be as Chris envisioned it?

Question 3: How do you feel about the statements "Hell is for those who can't forgive themselves," and "Hell is for those who don't know they're dead"?

Question 4: If you were going into the Gates of Hell, whom would you want by your side?

Question 5: If you went to hell to find someone you love, would you stay there with him or her if he or she would not come back with you?

Question 6: What do you think hell is really like? Do you agree with the film's depiction of hell, or do you think that it will be something else?

Have someone read aloud Psalm 139.

Question 7: Psalm 139 says that God will be with us even if we are in hell. How does this help you to understand what happens between Chris and Annie when he finds her in hell? (Chris wins Annie by convincing her to accept forgiveness and grace and by helping her focus on her love. Wherever love is present, God is present.)

Question 8: Do you think that even if people are in hell, it still might be possible for them to experience grace and be forgiven, as Annie was?

Question 9 (Optional): As Christians, we do not believe in reincarnation; but this film ends with Chris and Annie going back to start over with a new life. Why do you think they went back? (Possible answers might include but are not limited to the following: to experience falling in love with one another again, to work on aspects of their lives that they want to change, and to experience the joy and pain of physical existence one more time.)

> These sessions can be combined in a retreat format with "The Heavenly Retreat." from REEL TO REAL, Volume 2, Number 4. This retreat features *City of Angels, Defending Your Life, Ghost,* and *Always.*

Simon Birch

Two to Three Sessions

"Who knows? Perhaps you have come to the throne for just such a time as this."

Esther 4:14b

The wise mind will know the time and the way. For every matter has its time and way, although the troubles of mortals lie heavy upon them. Indeed, they do not know what is to be, for who can tell them how it will be? No one has power over the wind to restrain the wind, or power over the day of death.

Ecclesiastes 8:5b-8a

Even though you intended to do harm to me, God intended it for good.

Genesis 50:20

THEME Whether you believe that God's will governs every aspect of your life or that the Holy Spirit works through the serendipity of free will, one person's life can have great power to change the world.

PURPOSE Youth will explore the questions puzzling the main characters in the film: What is the purpose of my life? Why was I born different? Is God active in my life? Am I loved?

BACKGROUND *Simon Birch* (1998) is rated PG and is 113 minutes long.

CAUTIONS *Simon Birch* is rated PG for occasional strong language and scenes of death.

SYNOPSIS Two boys, Joe and Simon, best friends from birth, grow up in a small New England town. Simon Birch, unwanted by his parents, is unusually small in stature and hopes that there is a purpose to his life. Joe Wentworth is from a single-parent family and wonders who his father really is. Beginning narration states that Simon was a peculiar little disappointment to his parents from the day he was born. Both boys are active in the local Episcopal church; Simon is the bane of the Sunday school teacher's life but raises questions worthy of a seminarian. Simon is convinced from a very early age that he was born for a special reason and that he will be a hero. His faith in this and in God is very strong. He tells his friend Joe that God has a plan for everyone. The boys' lives radically change when Joe's mother dies in a freak accident after being struck on the temple by Simon's foul ball at a community Little League game. Simon and Joe break into their coach's office at school in an effort to determine if he is Joe's father. The boys are caught red handed, and the town police chief sentences them to community service (they must assist their minister with the annual 3rd graders retreat). After a disastrous Christmas pageant, Simon is banned from the retreat. When the 3rd graders and Joe leave for the retreat, Simon breaks into the church office and, by coincidence, discovers that Joe's father is their priest, Reverend Russell. Simon gets Ben Goodrich (the high school drama teacher and Rebecca Wentworth's last significant love interest) to take him to the retreat site to tell Joe, only to arrive as Reverend Russell is making his own confession to being Joe's father. On the way home, the church bus runs into an icy river. Joe and Simon rescue everyone on the bus. In saving the last and youngest child, Simon almost drowns and later dies due to complications.

MATERIALS

- *Simon Birch* video
- TV and VCR
- Flip chart paper
- Markers
- Masking tape
- Boom box
- CD or Tape of the song "Born to Be Wild," by Steppenwolf
- 3 or 4 Bibles
- Parcheesi games or other games of chance with dice

SESSION 1: ACCIDENT OF BIRTH?

Joe and Simon both seem to be accidents of birth. Between Simon's birth defects and near failure to thrive and Joe's lack of a known father (especially significant in a small town), they are drawn together in their specialness. Get the group to name circumstances or special physical or health concerns that might set a young person apart from the crowd. Examples might be Attention Deficit Disorder, Spina Bifida, Scoliosis, having parents of two different races or cultures, Cerebral Palsy, single-parent children, Muscular Dystrophy. Encourage the group to think of these and other special circumstances. Discuss how being different in any way often seems, at first, to be a liability but later can be a strength. The youth leader should make a list of

VIDEO VIEWING Begin with a prayer. Then watch *Simon Birch*. If you've decided to view selected clips, use the Video Viewing chart below as a guide.

Suggestion: Preview the film on the VCR that you will use with the program. Make note of these key scenes so you can fast forward during the program, using these approximate start-end times and your VCR counter.

Start-End	Event	Count
0:02–0:25	Joe's reflection about his friend	_____
0:07–0:10	Simon's birth and explanation of his family life	_____
0:22–0:23	Simon's talks about his belief that he will be a hero	_____
0:27–0:29	God has a plan for everyone, even Ben Goodrich	_____
0:32–0:34	Simon's outburst in church and the consequences	_____
0:37–00:39	Foul ball kills Rebecca Wentworth	_____
0:46–0:47	Joe's grief	_____
0:49–0:52	Joe's grandmother attempts to explain the gravity of his situation	_____
0:57–1:00	The big break in	_____
1:02–1:03	Ben rescues the offenders	_____
1:14–1:22	The Christmas play; Rev. Russell's chat with Simon	_____
1:24–1:25	Joe's outburst at Simon's father	_____
1:29–1:30	The second break in	_____
1:33–1:35	Rev. Russell confesses to Joe	_____
1:40–1:44	Bus wreck and rescue	_____
1:46–1:47	In the hospital: "You're a hero, Simon Birch."	_____

responses on a large sheet of paper to leave in the meeting room as a reference for future discussions about how to make people who are "different" feel loved and welcome.

RELAY RACE

Tape the posters to the floor (face down if the group normally meets in this room and will be hanging out there before the program begins) about 6 feet apart and about 20 feet from the starting line. Divide the group into 2, 3, or 4 teams, depending on the number of youth. Tell each team to line up behind the starting line. Give the first person in each line a marker. Explain that each team member will run down to their

poster, choose a personality from the left side and draw a line from the person to what he or she was "born to be," then run back, pass the marker to the next person in line, and go to the end of the line. The next person takes off as soon as he or she receives the hand off.

During the relay, play the oldie but goodie "Born to Be Wild," by Steppenwolf, or other appropriate frantic music. Tell the youth that you are going to play a tune. The race begins when the lyrics start in the song. The first team to finish the poster wins. The team that actually gets all the "born to be's" right wins too. Prizes? Tootsie Roll Pops® for everyone.

ACTIVITY: BORN TO BE

Before the session, choose a large activity room suitable for a relay race. Lay a masking tape ("starting line" on the floor at one end of the room/hall. Make a large poster answer sheet for each team with the following lists:

PERSON	CONTRIBUTION
Mariah Carey	Singer
John Glenn	American Astronaut/Senator
Sammy Sosa	Baseball Player
Leonardo DaVinci	Inventor/Scientist/Artist
Billy Graham	Preacher/Spiritual Leader
Gandhi	Reformer/National Leader/Peacemaker
Deion Sanders	Football Player/Baseball Player
Martin Luther King, Jr.	Civil Rights Leader/Minister
Picasso	Artist
Elizabeth Dole	Head of the Red Cross/Presidential Candidate
Mother Teresa	Missionary/Nobel Peace Prize Winner
Abraham Lincoln	President of the U.S.
Will Smith	Actor/Singer
Albert Einstein	Physicist/E=mc2
Jesus	Redeemer/Savior/Prince of Peace
Queen Latifah	Actress /Singer
Michael Jordan	Basketball Player
Stephen King	Writer
Barbara Walters	News Anchor/Interviewer
Amy Grant	Christian Singer

After the game, invite everyone to sit on the floor in a circle. Follow up the relay race with a discussion on the "Accident of Our Birth." Refer to Simon Birch and the accident of his birth, his birth defect(s), how it affected his personality and world view and his certainty that he was born to be a hero. End the session with the prayer that each person remember that we are all children of God, loved and accepted unconditionally. Any "accidents of our birth" are blessings to be embraced as merely that—accidents that have molded us into who we are, precious in God's sight.

SESSION 2: DOES GOD HAVE A PLAN FOR YOUR LIFE?

Most Christians answer this question in the affirmative. When some Christians answer yes, they mean that God plans even the minutia of a person's life or that there is a firm, divine step-by-step game plan for them. When others say yes, they believe that God plans for them to love and forgive in a world full of random action and chance, that God's will is carried out through their loving responses in the midst of the swirl of events around them.

Simon Birch says, "What does God have to do with coffee and donuts? Faith is not in a floor plan." Joe's grandmother tells him, "You have only yourself to depend on now." Ben Goodrich told the boys, "Maybe you are not ready for the truth."

ACTIVITY: THE BEST LAID PLANS

Divide the group into four teams. Give each group a Bible and the following list of verses or other Bible verses to look up. Ask the teams to answer the questions listed below.

Exodus 12:15-31
Genesis 22:1-14
Isaiah 6:1-9
Matthew 4:1-11
Luke 2:1-20
Esther 1:9-17

• How did plans change for the characters in these well known Bible stories? (Example: Joseph and Mary had to make a long unexpected trip to Bethlehem when she was close to giving birth, they have to find shelter quickly before the baby comes, they can't go home because of Herod and end up living in Egypt for two years, rich men show up out of the blue to give their baby gifts.)

- Are changes in plans chance happenings or part of God's plan? for us? for humankind?

SESSION 3: RANDOM CHANCE

After Simon's foul ball hits and kills Joe's mother, Joe's outburst is, "There are no accidents. There is no God. Stop trying to make sense of it all, 'cause you can't."

Begin the session with these statements or similar statements peculiar to your locale:

- When Hurricane Hugo struck Charleston, South Carolina, insurance companies called it an act of God.
- When an earthquake struck San Francisco during a World Series game, others also called this an act of God.
- During 1998, Hurricane Mitch blasted Central America. Governments in the region declared national disasters.
- When a meteor struck the Yucatan and wiped out the dinosaurs, historians and archeologists have called that a natural phenomenon.
- When Mrs. O'Leary's cow kicked over a lantern and burned down Chicago, the newspapers called it a catastrophe.

List and discuss other "acts of God" or natural events of random chance. Possible examples are tornadoes, hail storms, lighting strikes, shark attacks, snake bites, striking a deer on the highway, avalanches, Simon Birch's foul ball, mosquito bites, traffic accidents, cancer, droughts.

A practical arm of mathematics much used by gamblers, insurance companies, and casinos is the study of permutations and combinations. Divide the group into teams of four. Have each team play Parcheesi or another game of chance while they discuss these questions and also the probability or possibility that they will be struck by lighting on their way home from their meeting.

- When or how is God's will expressed through random chance?
- How does a person filled with the spirit react to the events or happenings of random chance or so called "acts of God" (see the list in Column 1)?

After about 20 or 30 minutes, or sooner before interest begins to wane, get everyone back together in a circle. Call out various scenes from *Simon Birch*. Ask the group to decide whether the examples given are: 1) a random chance occurrence [a deer running in front of a bus]; 2) An act of God [a foul ball hits and kills the most important person in Joe and Simon's life]; or 3) goof-ups [Simon gives in to the temptation to grope his classmate in the Christmas play].

Use the following questions or statements for more discussion, then close the session with prayer.

Question 1: What might Simon have meant by his statement and belief that "Everything happens for a reason"?

Question 2: Discuss the prayer (about going to heaven) that Simon said for Rebecca Wentworth and that Joe prayed for Simon years later.

Question 3: After the play Rev. Russell tells Simon, "We need a break from you." Simon says, "I want you to tell me God has a plan, please." Rev. Russell replies, "I can't." How would you describe this interchange in terms of faith, forgiveness, acceptance and redemption?

Question 4: Did God give Simon the desire to hold his breath for long periods of time, or did Simon's natural desire to excel at something become part of God's plan at the right time? (Christians will answer respond is different ways.)

Question 5: Is wondering about whether you have a purpose in life sophisticated or childish to think about?

Question 6: What is the symbolism of the three deer appearances? (Perhaps the first and third deer are a sign of God's presence of reassurance, the middle deer an act of God? random chance? goof-up?)

Question 7: When Ben Goodrich tells Simon and Joe, "Maybe you weren't ready for the truth." What did he mean? Maturity? Fear? Understanding? Ability to grapple with the consequences of knowledge? Other things?

Question 8: Discuss heroism, destiny and "God's plan" in terms of the outcome of the crash and how each character (Ben Goodrich, the bus driver, Joe Wentworth, the youngest child, Simon Birch) functioned or acted during the accident.

Question 9: During the opening credits, a grown-up Joe reflects that "Simon Birch is the reason I believe in God." Who or what has had this profound an influence on the lives of you? Your family? Your friends? A good teacher like Ben Goodrich? A public official? Others?

The Mask of Zorro

On the seventh day they rose early, at dawn, and marched around the city in the same manner seven times. It was only on that day that they marched around the city seven times. And at the seventh time, when the priests had blown the trumpets, Joshua said to the people, "Shout! For the LORD has given you the city." . . . So the people shouted, and the trumpets were blown. As soon as the people heard the sound of the trumpets, they raised a great shout, and the wall fell down flat; so the people charged straight ahead into the city and captured it.

Joshua 6:15-16, 20

PURPOSE Youth will uncover a message of hope for the landless and homeless peoples of our country and the world.

THEME Hidden behind the swashbuckling adventures of Zorro are multitudes of people who have been cheated out of land and livelihoods by a greedy few. This is also the message of the biblical Book of Joshua, an account of how a great hero took the Promised Land from a few wealthy city kings and gave it to landless peasants. Unfortunately, the problem of a wealthy few owning most of the earth's territory is still with us today, an injustice that prevents world peace from becoming a reality.

BACKGROUND The Mask of Zorro is 136 minutes long and is rated PG-13.

CAUTIONS The Mask of Zorro contains several violent fights, particularly toward the end. A man's severed head is displayed in a water jar. A scene containing partial nudity occurs near the beginning, and there is occasional mild swearing. Always preview movies, and send home a Student Movie Pass (parent consent form on the inside back cover) if you think that it is necessary.

SYNOPSIS The people of Alta California, a province of Mexico, have been under the domination of Spain's monarchy for 300 years. With the help of Zorro, the people rise against Spain to seek justice and control of their own land. Before the governor retreats in defeat, however, he imprisons Zorro and kidnaps Zorro's baby daughter. Twenty years later, Zorro (Don Diego de la Vega) escapes from prison just as Governor Montero returns to reclaim the land; and Zorro discovers that Montero has raised Elena, the kidnaped daughter, as his own. De la Vega trains an outlaw, Alejandro Murrieta, to take over as the new Zorro. Together they establish justice and give the land back to the people.

MATERIALS
- *The Mask of Zorro* video
- TV and VCR
- Large newsprint or a chalkboard and writing implements

USING THESE SESSIONS & ACTIVITIES

If you have time, show the entire video before beginning the discussion and activities. Review key scenes, if necessary, during activities that emphasize those scenes. If you have time only for clips, be prepared to provide an account of the missing story parts so that the narrative continuity is maintained.

DISCUSSING & LEARNING

Have someone read aloud Joshua 6:15-16, 20. Some of the youth may be familiar with the story (and song) of "Joshua Fit the Battle of Jericho." Say: "God told Joshua to take the people into the Promised Land after Moses died. It is likely that the Israelites joined with the poor peasants of the Promised Land and took the land away from the powerful city kings. In this way, the Book of Joshua tells a story much like Zorro's: God sided with the poor, weak, landless peasant farmers and sent them a hero to lead them to justice."

VIDEO VIEWING After an opening prayer, show *The Mask of Zorro*. If you only have time only for clips, key scenes are identified below in the Video Viewing chart. Use the chart for quickly locating these clips during discussion.

Suggestion: Preview the film on the VCR that you will use with the program. Make note of these key scenes so you can fast forward during the program, using these approximate start-end times and your VCR counter.

Start–End	Event	Count
0:00–0:09	Don Diego de la Vega (Zorro) saves three peasants from Montero.	_____
0:09–0:17	Montero avenges himself and kidnaps de la Vega's daughter.	_____
0:17–0:23	Alejandro Murrieta watches Captain Love kill his brother.	_____
0:23–0:29	Don Diego de la Vega escapes from prison.	_____
0:29–0:32	Montero returns with Elena.	_____
0:33–0:39	De la Vega discovers Alejandro in a cantina.	_____
0:39–0:42	Alejandro learns his skills in the training circle.	_____
0:57–1:00	Zorro learns to be a servant of the people.	_____
1:04–1:08	"Gentleman" Zorro gains access to Montero's villa.	_____
1:13–1:15	Montero shows the Dons his "vision" for the future of the land.	_____
1:15–1:20	Slaves serve the cruel Montero.	_____
1:28–1:30	Zorro learns to put aside his vengeance to help the people.	_____
1:43–1:46	The new Zorro must save the people.	_____
1:59–2:09	Two generations battle for justice.	_____

Question 1: Imagine that you are a poor farmer who must have at least forty acres of land to support your family. Now imagine that the governor has deeded thousands of acres to a rich friend. Most of that land lies useless, and your family is starving. Assuming that you had no power or voice in the government, what would you do? (There are few peaceful options. In the Joshua story, the escaped slaves from Egypt had to fight for the land with the help of Joshua, a heroic leader. The same is true in the story of Mexico's battle for independence against Spain. Today the same thing continues in Mexico, Brazil, and many other countries around the world. The Bible teaches us to look for peaceful options, but few people would willingly let their families starve so that a few rich land barons can live in luxury.)

Question 2: Can you identify scenes in *The Mask of Zorro* in which the situation described in Question 1 occurs? (In the opening scene, Don Montero hurriedly deeds the land to the wealthy dons before he escapes to Spain. Also, at about 1:13 into the film, Montero tells about his "vision" of the land again divided among the dons after he steals it from the Mexican rebel Santa Anna. Nowhere in his plans are the needs of the people considered. In fact, the people become his slave labor in the gold mine in the next scene, at about 1:15.)

Question 6: Some would say that the wars that occur over land ownership violate Christian principles of peace. Do you agree? (This is a difficult question. Remind youth that peace without justice is an incomplete picture of God's will. When all peaceful means end, some people feel that they must fight. As Christians, our duty is to protect the rights of the weak in order to prevent conflict.)

DESIGN A HERO FOR TODAY

In Spanish, the word *zorro* means "fox"; and Zorro had to be as sly and cunning as a fox in order to outwit the Spanish land-grabbers. Throughout history, there have been both real and fictional heroes who possessed special traits in order to lead people to salvation.

To begin this activity, list some real and fictional heroes on newsprint such as the following: Real—Jesus Christ, Joshua, Harriet Tubman; fictional—Robin Hood, Zorro. Ask the youth to add their own favorites, then make a list of heroic qualities shared by these people.

Ask: "If you had to design a hero to lead a group of landless peasants to justice and equality, what would he or she be like?" Then work as a group to design that hero. The design might be nothing more than a list of characteristics on newsprint; or a sketch or drawing may be added if there is artistic talent in your group. As you guide the youth in this activity, remind the youth that super hero qualities are not necessarily needed. After all, God often chose the least likely candidate to perform an important task. (For example, David, Israel's greatest king, was the youngest and weakest of many brothers.) The ability to lead, negotiate, and speak foreign languages would be very important. Bring God into the discussion, reminding the group that God changes and empowers people when they are working for God's Kingdom.

Question 3: How important do you think land ownership is to people in developing nations? (Many would be surprised to know that land ownership is critical to survival for millions around the world. Peasant farmers, who often hold no deeds to ancestral or family lands, are cheated out of their inheritances when their governments, which are sometimes unelected, sell the land to special interest groups. This is happening today in the rain forest, for example. Without land, people die. No food or clean water, no grazing pastures, no way to earn crops to sell. Some (for instance, in Africa) migrate to crowded cities, where they live in ghettoes and shanty towns. AIDS and other health problems plague these poorest of the poor.)

Show the clip where Zorro learns to be a servant of the people.

Question 4: The scene you have just viewed is a wonderful one, filled with action and humor. In light of what you have learned so far in this discussion, what is the most important thing said in this scene? (Although answers may vary, many would agree that it is de la Vega's statement that Zorro should be a servant of the people, because everything the original Zorro did was on their behalf. Here he is trying to show Alejandro, the new Zorro, that there are higher motivations than personal revenge for what he is about to do.)

Question 5: Most viewers find this film to be highly enjoyable and entertaining. How does your new knowledge of the motivation behind Zorro's deeds contribute to your opinion about it? (For many, this knowledge adds depth to an already excellent feature. In addition, knowing that the story is strikingly similar in theme to the Book of Joshua gives Christian viewers an even clearer insight.)

> "And I will give to you, and to your offspring after you, the land where you are now an alien, all the land of Canaan, for a perpetual holding; and I will be their God."
> God said to Abraham, "As for you, you shall keep my covenant, you and your offspring after you throughout their generations."
> Genesis 17:8-9

> Then Joshua blessed him, and gave Hebron to Caleb son of Jephunneh for an inheritance. So Hebron became the inheritance of Caleb son of Jephunneh the Kenizzite to this day, because he wholeheartedly followed the LORD, the God of Israel.
> Joshua 14:13-14

A QUESTION OF OWNERSHIP

The Genesis Scripture above is one of several references to a covenant between God and humankind in the Bible. Any covenant between God and humans will involve two things: first, a gift from God, the giver of all life; second, obedience by humans. The agreement in this passage involves the gift of land. To retain the gift, the Israelites must obey God. One way they must obey is to respect the land and share it with all, for the land is the key to life. (The first thing Joshua did when the fighting was over was to divide the land among all the people.) The Joshua 14 Scripture is an example of one family group's gift of land. Notice what it is called: an inheritance. People do not own the land; God owns the land. People hold it then pass it on to the next generation. Propose the following idea to the group: If we think of our possessions, including land, as God's possessions to be held in safe keeping for the next generation, what would change in the way we live our lives? (There are many directions in which this discussion can proceed. Some possibilities: Environmental pollution would be a major concern. Also, if something we "own" truly belongs to God, we are more likely to be willing to share it with the less fortunate out of a grateful heart. For example, if God owns our money, would we really spend most of it foolishly; or would we think before spending?)

ACTION POINT: A QUESTION OF VISION

As is seen in the clip labeled "Montero shows the dons his vision for the future of the land," greedy landholders have a clear vision of what they want. Unfortunately, peasant farmers often are so caught up in the daily grind of survival that they do not have time or energy to look beyond the moment. What they need is others who will give them their vision. Often, missionaries do exactly that. Like a doctor healing a blind person, they open people's eyes to their rights and help them organize into groups to claim their land.

If you want to take this lesson to the next step, assign some members of your youth group to find and report on as many organizations as possible that dedicate their time and gifts to the homeless or landless, both in this country and around the world. (You may want to consider American family farmers, whose land is being bought up by large agricultural corporations.) Possible resources for interviews are your pastor, your church's mission leader, your community's Habitat for Humanity liaison. And don't forget the Internet. After the reports, discuss ways in which your group can help through one of these organizations.

CLOSING PRAYER

Pray a prayer such as the following: "Dear God, who gave us all that we have, we often forget that it all still belongs to you. In the same spirit of love that you have for us, teach us to give generously to those in need. Give us eyes to see those in need, ears to hear their cries, and hearts open to respond. Amen."

For we do not proclaim ourselves; we proclaim Jesus Christ as Lord and ourselves as your slaves for Jesus' sake. For it is the God who said, "Let light shine out of darkness," who has shone in our hearts to give the light of the knowledge of the glory of God in the face of Jesus Christ. But we have this treasure in clay jars, so that it may be made clear that this extraordinary power belongs to God and does not come from us.

2 Corinthians 4:5-7

THEME
God wants us to discover who we are and what we are called to be through love and grace.

PURPOSE
We must learn to love ourselves and see ourselves as unique, individual creations of a loving God. Only then can we learn to love one another unconditionally as Christ loved us.

BACKGROUND
Mulan (1998) is 88 minutes long and is rated G.

CAUTIONS
Mulan dresses as a man to take her father's place in the army. There are a few remarks made about cross-dressing; and several of the soldiers go skinny-dipping, but no nudity is shown. Most of the violence is done off screen. The villain is fairly intense by Disney standards, but there is nothing that has not been seen before. As always, be sure to preview the entire movie before showing it to your youth.

SYNOPSIS
Pha-Mulan, a young girl, takes the place of her aging, crippled father when her country goes to war. She assumes the identity of a male and trains with the army. When Mulan's army is attacked, it is Mulan's quick intelligence that saves them all. She is injured, and her secret is discovered. She is thrown out and left behind. When the emperor's palace is attacked, it is Mulan who leads her friends in an undercover mission to rescue the emperor. In the end, Mulan is recognized for her bravery. She receives a position of honor in the emperor's staff and returns home to honor her father.

USING THE SESSIONS & ACTIVITIES

The *Mulan* retreat is designed to be used in three sessions. Each session is preceded by viewing one segment of the movie. Each segment deals with a specific theme. Viewing the entire movie and then discussing it in one session would require a lengthy time slot. Several sessions are recommended if you view this film in a situation other than a retreat format.

MATERIALS

- *Mulan* video
- TV and VCR
- Several large sheets of paper or a roll of butcher's paper
- Markers
- Paper plates
- Scissors
- Pieces of elastic or long rubber bands
- Stapler
- Old newspapers or enough used paper to make lots of paper wads

SESSION 1: THE MASK

THEME We all wear masks of one kind or another. It is important to not let society tells us who we should be but to become who we are in the sight of God.

Begin with a prayer. then view the first 25:00 minutes of *Mulan,* stopping the tape when Mushu the dragon leaves the village to protect Mulan.

ICE BREAKER

Break the youth into small groups. Hand out the paper plates and ask the youth to draw a mask of themselves as they believe others see them or as they think the world wants them to be. Have scissors on hand to cut out eye holes. Make sure that the youth have their name on the mask somewhere so that the masks can be redistributed later.

DISCUSSING & LEARNING

Take turns talking about how the youth drew their masks.

Ask them questions such as
Question 1: Is this how the world sees you, or is this how you think the world wants you to be?

Question 2: What does society expect of teenagers today?

Question 3: How do you think that society and its expectations have changed since your parents were teens?

Collect the masks and place them aside. You will get these back out in Session 3, but don't tell the youth.

Question 4: Mulan is painted in a sort of mask so that she will look like all of the others. What are the expectations of Mulan's family as she prepares to see the matchmaker.

At this point you can bring up lines from the song such as:

"With good fortune and a great hairdo."
> or
"With good breeding and a tiny waist"
> or
"A sows ear into a silk purse."

Question 5: In what ways is our society's expectation similar to Mulan's village?

In Mulan's song she sings: "Look at me—I am not meant to play this part. If I were myself, I would break my family's heart," and "When will my reflections show who I am inside."

Have someone read aloud 2 Corinthians 4:5-7.

Question 6: What treasures are inside Mulan?

Question 7: Why do you think the writers had Mulan wipe off half the make-up?

Question 8: Why does Mulan feel like two people? Can you think of a time when you have felt this way?

Question 9: How do we change ourselves in order to fit in?

Question 10: What does it take to be part of the popular group at your school?

Question 10: What other masks do we wear in our lives?

Question 12: What treasures do you have inside that you don't share very often?

Remind the youth that the film's tag line is "The flower that blooms in diversity is the most rare and beautiful of all." Mention that Mulan's father refers to the "late blossom."

Have someone read aloud Matthew 13:1-9 (the parable of the sower).

Hang up three sheets of large paper or a large piece of the butcher paper. Write the following three headings at the top: *Birds, Rocky Soil, Good Soil.*

Ask the youth first to talk about where the "birds" are in their lives. Write their answers under the *Birds* heading.

Question 13: What are the things that can kick you back before you can even get started?

Question 14: What are the things that discourage you the most? (You will probably get answers about parents, school, peers. Write all these down.

Then ask the youth about people they know or have heard about who blossomed quickly and then faded away. They may be people the kids know from school. Offer the names of celebrities or groups who seemed to have disappeared. Offer suggestions such as young actor River Phoenix or comedian John Belushi, who were at the peek of their careers and then lost it all

because of bad decisions. List these things under *Rocky Soil.*

Finally ask the youth to name all of the things that are "good soil" in their lives. These do not have to be things they already have. They can be things that they believe will make good soil or things that should make good soil.

Question 15: What kind of seed is Mulan? (Point out that Mulan's family prays a lot. The first time we see Mulan's father, he is in prayer. The last thing Mulan does before she runs away is pray.)

Question 16: What are Mulan's motivations to take her father's place?

Say something such as: "Mulan's soil is good. She will grow and be strong and blossom." Then say a prayer, praying for the youth in the group, for their families, and for all of the things that make them strong. Pray that God will guide the youth as they grow and become part of the Creator's garden.

SESSION 2: ROLE REVERSALS

Begin the session with prayer. Then view the second portion of Mulan (0:25 to 0:50). Stop the video after the army sings the song: "A Girl worth Fighting for."

PURPOSE The youth will learn about myths about the opposite sex, about how to get along with others, and about perseverance during hard times of trial.

LEARNING ACTIVITY

If possible, clear the room of chairs or move them all to the side of the room. Take two large sheets of paper and write the words *True* and *False* on them. Tape the sheets of paper on the walls that are opposite each other. Have the youth stand in the middle of the room.

Say: "I'm going to read a series of statements. When I say go, run and stand by the wall corresponding with how you feel about the statement.

(NOTE: If you are working with a smaller group, this activity works great with a "true couch" and a "false couch." The youth must all be on the couch together. There cannot be standing beside it.)

While you are playing this game, select individual youth to speak their opinions. Don't allow too much time for discussion for each question. This game gets bogged down if it doesn't keep moving.

- After all is said and done, it is still basically a man's world.
- The man should be the primary bread winner in the home.
- The woman is the one better suited to be the child-raiser.

- It is the guy's responsibility to ask for the date.
- It is always the guy's responsibility to pay for a date regardless of who asked whom out.
- In the home, cooking and laundry is women's work.
- Housework should be shared equally no matter who makes more money or who works more hours.
- Women are the brains of a relationship, and men are the brawn.
- Men suffer from peer pressure more than women do.
- Women put more pressure on themselves than men do.
- Men are naturally better leaders than women.
- There are no women leaders in the Bible. (Save this as your last question and then pick up the Bible and read Judges 4:4-7.)

DISCUSSING & LEARNING

Mulan cannot understand what it is like to be "a man." The song compares men to a raging river" yet at night the men go off on their own to pray.

- Ask the guys in your group: "What is the one thing women most misunderstand about men?"

- Ask the girls in your group: "What is the one thing men most misunderstand about women?"

Then ask the whole group:

Question 1: How do men and women approach problem solving differently?

Question 2: How do men and women approach relationships differently?

Question 3: Do you think that there is any task that men or women are more naturally suited for?

Question 4: Do you think that God had a separate plan for men and women?

Have the youth break into small groups. Have someone read aloud Phillipians 3:12-13.

Question 5: Captain Shang fires an arrow at the top of the pole. He hands the stones to Yao and names them *Strength* and *Discipline*. He says, "You will need both." How does Mulan reach the arrow? Was that cheating? **Question 6:** At the beginning of the training, Mulan cannot keep up. She continues to fail but keeps getting up. Being sent home by Captain Shang only fuels her desire to fight harder. How would you apply the verse from Phillipians to Mulan's situation?

Question 7: If you were to name two more weights what would you call them? Remember that they must be used together or they can work against you. (Possible examples are intelligence and emotion, speed and endurance, creativity and regulation, faith and reason.)

Say a prayer, praying for guidance in all friendships. Thank God for all of the things that make us different. Ask God to open our minds to the truth and to help us let go of the stereotypes we've come to accept of one another.

SESSION 3: MASK OFF!

PURPOSE Youth will learn about standing up for what they believe in. They will discuss taking off the masks they wear for others and accepting and loving who they are.

DISCUSSING & LEARNING

Give the youth their masks, and let them attach elastic or rubber bands to them.

View the final segment of *Mulan*.

Ask for volunteers to read aloud the following Scripture passages: 1 Timothy 3:8-16 (leadership), Matthew 12:19-21 (qualities of leadership), Matthew 20:26-28 (leaders must be servants).

Say: "During the battle, it is Mulan who saves her friends. Captain Shang's action would not have saved them. When Shang and his men try to break down the door of the palace, it is Mulan that they follow. She is a leader. Her gender does not matter."

Question 1: What do the Scriptures say about being a leader?

Question 2: In what way does Mulan possess these qualities that Captain Shang does not?

Question 3: Is it more difficult for a woman to be accepted as a CEO or for a man to be accepted as a nurturing parent?

LEARNING ACTIVITY

Have the youth break into small groups. Hand out the sheets of newspaper or used sheets of paper.

Question 1: Which character is most like you?

Question 2: This is one of the few Disney films in which the villain does not get a song. How many other "villain songs" can you sing? Why do you think *Mulan's* villain does not get a song?

Question 3: When Mulan leaves, we see the eyes on one of the ancestor's statue "blink" and Grandma wakes up, saying: "Mulan is gone." Later we see the ancestor wake up to Grandma's prayer. Is it possible that Grandma can communicate with the ancestors because she is going to be with them soon?

Ask for a volunteer. Have him or her stand in front of the group and put on the mask that he or she created earlier. (Remember this is the mask that represents who others see or who others want them to be.)

Have the youth make paper wads and take turns throwing them at the youth in the mask. The masked youth may duck, catch, or hit the paper wads out of the way. Let the throwers start throwing simultaneously. Eventually, the masked person won't be able to keep up with the barrage.

Have the person remove the mask and try again. He or she might get better at defending himself or herself against the barrage.

Gather the group and have volunteers read the following Scriptures: 1 Corinthians 3:10-17 (being tested by fire), 2 Corinthians 5:16-18 (being a new creation).

Say: "Mulan was not an honorable bride. Mulan tried to be a man, but there was no way that she could do that. In the end of the movie, Mulan faces Shan-Yu alone. She is a girl with a sword. It is in this one moment that Mulan becomes who she is. Up until this moment, she was either unsure of herself or trying to please everyone else. It is only when we make the choice to be a child of God that we can become everything God wants us to be."

Gather for a final prayer, saying a prayer such as: "God in heaven, help us take off the masks that keep us from seeing you. Help us take off the masks that hide who we are. Let our faces and our lives reflect your light. Help us to weather the storms of our lives and know that you make us stronger each day. Help us be leaders by first being servants. Help us to be your children. Amen."

GAME: CHANGE

Get a full suit of men's clothing (pants, shoes, shirt, jacket) and a suit of women's clothing (dress, shoes, wig, purse). Place the clothes on two chairs. Divide your group into two teams, guys against girls. Have a relay race.

The guys must run down; put on the dress, purse, and wig; and then run to the nearest female counselor and ask: "Does this dress make me look fat?" Then he must return all of the items to the chair and tag the next guy in line. The girls must run to the chair; and after dressing, run to the nearest male counselor and punch him in the arm, saying: "How 'bout them Broncos" (or whatever sports team is in your city).

BIBLICAL FORTUNES

Have a full Chinese dinner. A folding table with the legs folded under it is just the right height for sitting on the floor to eat. Stop by a local Chinese restaurant and ask for some chopsticks to use. At the end of the dinner, serve fortune cookies. Prior to the meal, copy the Biblical Fortunes below. Clip out the verses and replace the fortunes in store-bought fortune cookies. This will require some patience. If patience or time is lacking or if fortune cookies are difficult to find, try putting the fortunes into the middle of a sandwich cookie such as an Oreo®.

Too much pride can put you to shame. It is wiser to be humble.—Proverbs 11:2-3 (CEV)	What you gain by doing evil won't help you at all, but being good can save you from death. —Proverbs 10:2 (CEV)
When God is angry, money won't help you.— Proverbs 11:4 (CEV)	Laziness leads to poverty; hard work makes you rich.—Proverbs 10:4 (CEV)
It's stupid to say bad things about your neighbors. If you are sensible, you will keep quiet. —Proverbs 11:12 (CEV)	Hatred stirs up trouble; love overlooks the wrongs that others do.—Proverbs 10:12 (CEV)
If you do your job well, you will work for a ruler and never be a slave.—Proverbs 22:29 (CEV)	If you have good sense, it will show when you speak. But if you are stupid, you will be beaten with a stick.—Proverbs 10:13 (CEV)
Giving an honest answer is a sign of true friendship.—Proverbs 24:26 (CEV)	A kind answer soothes angry feelings, but harsh words stir them up.—Proverbs 15:1 (CEV)
The right word at the right time is like precious gold set in silver.—Proverbs 25:11 (CEV)	It isn't smart to get drunk! Drinking makes a fool of you and leads to fights.—Proverbs 20:1 (CEV)
Good news from far away refreshes like cold water when you are thirsty.—Proverbs 25:25 (CEV)	You may think you have won your case in court, until your opponent speaks.—Proverbs 18:17 (CEV)
The lifestyle of good people is like sunlight at dawn that keeps getting brighter until broad daylight. —Proverbs 4:18 (CEV)	It's stupid and embarrassing to give an answer before you listen.—Proverbs 18:13 (CEV)
Carefully guard your thoughts because they are the source of true life.—Proverbs 4:23 (CEV)	Children who curse their parents will go to the land of darkness long before their time. —Proverbs 20:20 (CEV)

THE FINE PRINT

Q I understand that motion pictures are protected by federal copyright laws. Do these copyright laws apply to showing movies in our church youth group?

A Yes. Under the law, for-profit and nonprofit organizations are required to have a public performance license to show movies, which include purchased and rental videocassettes.

Q How does my church obtain rights to show full-length films and film clips for youth group and other Christian education purposes?

A You need to obtain a public performance license (sometimes called a site or umbrella license) to show movies on home video publicly, even for educational purposes. An umbrella license can be granted by The Motion Picture Licensing Corporation. The MPLC's Church Desk handles these requests. Contact Harald Bauer, Executive Vice President, at 800-515-8855 (fax 203-270-8830).

Q What is an umbrella license and what does it allow the church to do?

A An umbrella license is a 12-month license purchased by your church that enables you to use copyrighted films of your choice for preaching and teaching. If your church purchases an umbrella license, you may use entire videos or clips not only in your youth group with REEL TO REAL, but your pastor may use clips with sermons.

Q How much will an umbrella license cost?

A Generally, the umbrella license costs $95 for a 12-month period.

Q Are there any less expensive alternatives?

A Yes. Many denominations—through conferences, jurisdictions, dioceses, and other structures—already have public performance license agreements for their churches. Under these agreements, the church office negotiates with the MPLC a much lower rate per church. If your church's jurisdiction has an umbrella license for its churches, your church can qualify for the lower rate. If you're not sure, call your church's jurisdictional offices and ask whether an umbrella license agreement exists or is being pursued.

Q Without an umbrella license, are there ways to incorporate current film and REEL TO REAL in our youth group study?

A Yes. Oftentimes a movie featured in REEL TO REAL is still playing at the theaters or at the "dollar theater." So your group can pay admission price, see the movie during an outing, and discuss the REEL TO REAL session afterward or during another group time.

Another idea is to check out the Coming Attractions on the back cover of REEL TO REAL. Many of those movies are still playing in local theaters. You can make a youth outing of the movie and then discuss it when the next REEL TO REAL comes out.

Q Are there other restrictions, even if we purchase an umbrella license?

A Yes. You may only use pre-recorded videos, such as those purchased legally by an individual or rented from video stores or the public library.

You may not dub selected clips on another cassette to show to your group—the clip must be cued from the original pre-recorded tape. No license exists for showing movies taped from television or cable.

If you have any questions about your legal rights, call The Motion Picture Licensing Corporation at 800-515-8855.

THE COPYRIGHT LAW

- The Copyright Act grants to the copyright owner the exclusive right, among others, "to perform the copyrighted work publicly" (Section 106).

- The rental or purchase of a home videocassette does not carry with it the right "to perform the copyrighted work publicly" (Section 202).

- Home videocassettes may be shown, without a license, in the home to "a normal circle of family and its social acquaintances" (Section 101) because such showings are not "public."

- Home videocassettes may also be shown, without a license, in certain narrowly defined "face-to-face teaching activities" (Section 110.1) because the law makes a specific, limited exception for such showing. *There are no other exceptions.*

- All other showings of home videocassettes are illegal unless they have been authorized by license. Even "performances in 'semipublic' places such as clubs, lodges, factories, summer camps, and schools are 'public performances' subject to copyright control" (Senate Report No. 94-473, page 60; House Report No. 94-1476, page 64).

- Institutions, organizations, companies, or individuals wishing to engage in non-home showings of home videocassettes must secure licenses to do so—regardless of whether an admission or other fee is charged (Section 501). This legal requirement applies equally to profit-making organizations and nonprofit institutions (Senate Report No. 94-473, page 59; House Report No. 94-1476, page 62).